The Heart of an Addict

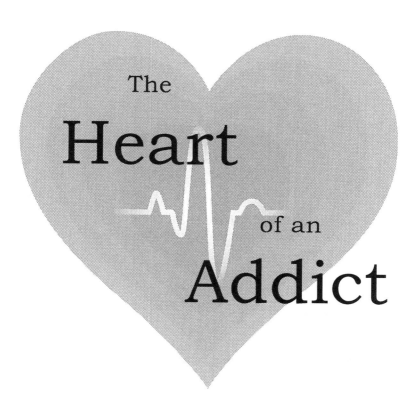

The

Heart

of an

Addict

David L. Hain

COACHWHIP PUBLICATIONS
Landisville, Pennsylvania

PUBLISHER'S DATA

The Heart of an Addict, © 2007, David L. Hain
Published by Coachwhip Publications. All rights reserved.
CoachwhipBooks.com

ISBN 1-930585-43-8
ISBN-13 978-1-930585-43-0

Scripture taken from the New King James Version.
© 1982 by Thomas Nelson, Inc.

Image credits, © respectively:
Front cover, Sharon Bogner
Back cover and title page, Valerij Kalyuzhnyy

Contents

Acknowledgements

I am forever thankful for the love and forgiveness of my Lord and Savior Jesus Christ. He is the light who is my life.

I also thank Him for my loving wife Shawn and two fine young sons Jordan and Isaac who bring God's love and joy into my life in huggable, laughable, memorable ways.

Introduction

When God chose a new king for Israel to replace Saul, He sent His prophet Samuel to anoint the one He chose. As Samuel met with Jesse and his sons, Samuel was impressed with Eliab, the firstborn of Jesse. But the Lord spoke to Samuel, "Do not look at his appearance or at his physical stature, because I have refused him. For the Lord does not see as man sees; for man looks at the outward appearance, but the Lord looks at the heart." (1 Samuel 16:7)

Most of us who have been hurt by the addictive lifestyle of a loved one find it almost impossible to look beyond their appearance and actions to see their heart. Our hearts have been broken, our dreams have vanished and our lives have been torn and tattered by the never-ending stream of lies and broken promises. We've spent countless hours praying, crying, and hoping that our loved one would come to his or her senses like the Prodigal Son and return home.

But God's Word is sure. He calls us to look at their heart. "As in water face reflects face, so a man's heart reveals the man." (Proverbs 27:19) In the same way that God wants us to look at their heart, His call on my life and our ministry has been to find Jesus in the heart of addicts! Throughout this book I will share the heart of many addicts, in their own words, as they shared their heart with me. Whenever you see this drawing,

stop and pray. Ask God to touch and change your heart to be able to see the heart of an addict.

God assured us that everyone caught in the bondage of addiction is His child! As my wife and I began to minister to addicts in Philadelphia, PA, God called us to walk with the loving heart of a father, of the Father, running to the Prodigal in love. Our ministry was not to take Jesus to the streets, the abandoned homes, and the crackhouses, but to find Jesus there!

Jesus said to His disciples, "for I was hungry and you gave Me food; I was thirsty and you gave Me drink; I was a stranger and you took Me in; I was naked and you clothed Me; I was in prison and you came to Me." In response to His disciples' questioning and bewilderment with these statements, Jesus replied, "Assuredly, I say to you, inasmuch as you did it to one of the least of these My brethren, you did it to Me." (Matthew 25:35-40)

So how do we find Jesus in the addicts? How do we find Jesus in midst of their life of fear, lies, deception, shame, guilt, paranoia, theft, lawlessness, hopelessness, and helplessness? We try to look at their heart. We look at addiction as a spiritual battle, not simply a reflection of someone's bad choices or decisions. It is a battle for the very soul of men, women, and children all around the world! The devil's desire is to lure as many people as possible into his trap!

People caught in the snare of addiction of any type—alcohol, drugs, pornography, lust, sex, anorexia, bulimia, over-eating, cutting, gambling, materialism, shopping, chocolate, soap operas, etc.—understand the bondage that addiction brings. Some of you may be thinking, "He just included me in that list and I'm not an addict!" My definition of addiction is engaging in impulsive or compulsive behavior even though we know the consequences. In other words the draw of the behavior is greater than our ability to say no.

Jesus said, "Most assuredly, I say to you, whoever commits sin is a slave of sin." (John 8:34) Addicts know how it feels to be a slave to their addiction. God's call to His Church is to bring the Truth which sets the captives free. His Word brings knowledge of the Truth which brings freedom from the dominion of sin. The promise of Jesus is sure. "If you abide in My word, you are My disciples indeed. And you shall know the truth and the truth shall make you free." (John 8:31-32)

Are you willing to let God bring His freedom through you? We are called to be people who are "speaking the truth in love." (Ephesians 4:15) We are called to speak correction with humility so "God perhaps will grant them repentance, so that they may know the truth, and that they may come to their senses and escape the snare of the devil, having been taken captive by him to do his will." (2 Timothy 2:25-26)

If your answer is "Yes," this book is an attempt to reveal the heart of many addicts I have had the blessing to call my friends in our years of ministry. It is my earnest prayer that God will touch your heart and mind the way He touched mine, because He is the only answer to addiction!

1

The Battle
for a Heart

"My Childhood"
Gregory Williams

My childhood was dim, no light at all,
Full of pain and sadness as I recall.
Have you seen my childhood?

My mother was a junkie, she was always high.
The truth wasn't in her, she was full of lies.
Have you seen my childhood?

My father an alcoholic, but he was never there.
Maybe he didn't love me or just didn't care.
Have you seen my childhood?

When I was mischievous, I was whipped like a slave.
The pain I felt I'll take to my grave.
Have you seen my childhood?

Mayhem and chaos day after day
Quite often I hit my knees to pray.
Feeling lonely and scared, crying night after night
Looking towards God for open insight.
Have you seen my childhood?

My mother died at forty but I didn't feel free.
You have no idea what it's like being me.
Have you seen my childhood?

My father died at forty three, but still no relief.
I barely knew the man, so my mourning was brief.
Have you seen my childhood?

Now I'm all grownup, but my mind's not intact.
Because I have a dilemma, it being crack!
Have you seen my childhood?

I'm constantly confused and I don't know what to do.
I've seen my childhood.
Have you?

Can you hear Greg's heart? If you met Greg, would you be able to see his heart? Too often we judge by outward appearance or actions and never see beneath the surface. Greg's outward appearance was the green uniform that all men incarcerated at the county jail wore. Greg's heart was the heart of a man struggling both with the emotional pain of his past and his present painful battle with an addiction to crack cocaine.

Greg's story is similar to that of many men and women I met on the streets of Philadelphia and other cities and prisons around the United States. Greg's story could be heard in any city, town, village, or rural area anywhere in the world. It is a story of bondage to addiction and addiction is the same all over the world. Not all of the stories are ones birthed in a painful childhood. Some are stories of experimentation, partying, or rebellion against parents, rules, and society's expectations. Some are stories of searching for truth, meaning, acceptance, or just fitting in. Some stories begin with pain medication given after a work injury or surgery. Some stories begin with a tragic or painful occurrence such as a death in the family, a divorce, or being fired from a job. But, in each of the stories, the high that came from the addictive behavior was the escape from pain, anger, frustration, low self-esteem, or boredom with present circumstances or situations.

That high is counterfeit! It may be effective for an hour, evening, or weekend, but the next morning brings feelings of shame and guilt. The true high is the love of God the Father and the hope of His Son, Jesus Christ. When we experience the true high, the next morning brings peace and joy!

But the battle is real! Addicts have heard the words that brought discouragement, despair and depression. In our desperation to try to bring them to their senses, we scream out words of judgment and condemnation. "You're no good!" "You'll never amount to anything!" "You have the choice to just stop!" "You're the black sheep of the family!" "How could you do this to me?" "Don't you love me or your own children?"

In response, the accuser of the saints, Satan, whispers, "You don't have to listen to them." "You know how to silence their words." "Forget about them and get high." And our secular treatment society proclaims, "Once an addict always an addict." "You have a chemical imbalance; here's another drug that will help you." "You have the disease of addiction."

This belief was reflected as a psychologist told a Lancaster County, PA, courtroom at the sentencing of a man convicted of sexually assaulting a young boy.[1] "He knew what he was doing was wrong and even cried to himself after the acts, but his behavior was compulsive and he could not control himself until legal involvement occurred. He won't stop. The behavior may be suppressed for a few years, but it will return. The risk is for life. It's not a curable condition."

The man's defense attorney stated, "I've seldom encountered a defendant with this level of remorse." But the judge concluded, "You have an illness, an uncontrollable illness. What you've done is despicable, and you should live with that for the rest of your life."

I understand that some of you may be uneasy right now. Yes, I've included THE addiction that makes many of us uneasy. But addiction is addiction! The battle is spiritual!

The Bible assures us that we know the Great Physician and He is in the healing business! We stand on the Truth of the

Bible. "Therefore, if anyone is in Christ, he is a new creation; old things have passed away; behold, all things have become new. Now all things are of God, who has reconciled us to Himself through Jesus Christ, and has given us the ministry of reconciliation." (2 Corinthians 5:17-18)

God is calling His Church to carry His message of Truth into the lie of addiction. His Truth can and does bring freedom to people caught in bondage to addiction. The blood of Jesus Christ reconciles all of us who were caught in sin to our Father. Are you willing to walk in the ministry of reconciliation to addicts?

To answer God's call, we need to step out of our comfort zone. We need to open our hearts and minds to believe God's Word and not just things that scholars and experts have said. We need to be willing to risk disappointment and heartache when an addict with whom we enter into relationship has a slip or relapses. Many addicts have told me, "It feels like no one really cares." Are you willing to care enough to share with an addict how you cast your cares on the One who cares for you?

2

The Heart on Heroin or Other Drugs

The Psalm of The Addict[1]

"An unknown dope addict, lost in the dream world of heroin, wrote the following:

"King Heroin is my Shepherd, I shall always want, He maketh me to lie down in the gutters. He leadeth me beside the troubled waters. He destroyeth my soul. He leadeth me in the paths of wickedness for the effort's sake. Yea, I shall walk through the valley of poverty and will fear all evil for thou, Heroin, art with me. Thy needle and capsule try to comfort me. Thou strippest the table of groceries in the presence of my family. Thou robbest my head of reason. My cup of sorrow runneth over. Surely heroin addiction shall stalk me all the days of my life and I will dwell in the House of the Damned forever.

"This typewritten psalm was found by a Long Beach police officer in a telephone booth. On the back of the card was handwritten this postscript:

"Truly this is my psalm. I am a young woman, 20 years of age, and for the past year and one half I have been wandering down the nightmare of the junkie. I want to quit taking dope and I try but I can't. Jail didn't cure me. Nor did hospitalization help me for long. The doctor told my family it would have been

better, and indeed kinder, if the person who first got me hooked
on dope had taken a gun and blown my brains out. And I wish
to God she had. My God how I do wish it."

Can you hear this young woman's heart? If you met her, would you be able to see her heart? Many times when we see a young woman who is addicted to heroin, we turn away in horror or disgust! We react to the outward appearance—bone-skinny and hardened by life on the streets. We forget that this young woman is someone's daughter! We forget that this young woman is also God's daughter!

Some of you are thinking, "I wouldn't know what to say if I ever met someone like her on the streets." Others are thinking, "It wouldn't be safe for me to go to the neighborhoods where a woman like her would be." We struggle at the thought of God calling us to go and speak His words in the midst of the neighborhoods caught in addiction or to those incarcerated for crimes committed to support their addiction. But all the time the enemy is not short for words and has an army of eager troops spreading his promises!

 However, if the devil and his henchmen had to tell the truth about heroin, here's what they would say.

Miss Heroin

So now Little Man you've grown tired of grass,
L.S.D., acid, cocaine, and hash.
And someone pretending to be a true friend
Said, "I'll introduce you to Miss Heroin."

Well Honey, before you start fooling with me,
Just let me inform you of how it will be.
For I will seduce you and make you my slave.
I've sent men much stronger than you to their graves.
You think you could never become a disgrace

And end up so addicted to poppy seed waste.
So you'll start inhaling me one afternoon;
You'll take me into your arms very soon.

And once I have entered deep down in your veins,
The craving will nearly drive you insane.
You'll need lots of money (as you have been told)
For darling, I'm much more expensive than gold.

You'll swindle your mother and, just for a buck,
You'll turn into something vile and corrupt.
You'll mug and you'll steal for my narcotic charm,
And feel contentment when I'm in your arms.

The day when you realize the monster you've grown,
You'll solemnly promise to leave me alone.
If you think that you've got the mystical knack,
Then, sweetie, just try getting me off your back.

The vomit, the cramps, your gut tied in a knot,
The jangling nerves screaming for just one more shot.
The hot chills, the cold sweat, the withdrawal pains
Can only be saved by my little white grains.

There's no other way, and there's no need to look;
For deep down inside, you will know you are hooked.
You'll desperately run to the pusher and then,
You'll welcome me back to your arms once again.

And when you return (just as I foretold!)
I know that you'll give me your body and soul.
You'll give up your morals, your conscience, your heart
And you will be mine until death do us part!

Anonymous

If Jesus Christ were walking the streets of your town, city, or country right now, I believe He would be on those streets with men and women caught in the snare of addiction. As He heard their words of hopelessness, His heart would be moved with compassion. As He heard the snickering words of doom from Satan's lips, He would send out His call to action.

But how do we get that same compassion? And if we get it, what do we do with our fear of addicts, those neighborhoods, and convicts? How do we overcome our fear and respond to His call to action? As we grow in understanding of the hearts of addicts, I believe God will fill our hearts with His compassion. God calls His Church to love addicts. "Beloved, let us love one another, for love is of God; and everyone who loves is born of God and knows God." "There is no fear in love, but perfect love casts out fear." "And this commandment we have from Him; that he who loves God must love his brother also." (1 John 4:7,18,21)

Men, women, and children in bondage to addiction are our brothers and sisters. They were created by the same God who created us. Through the expression of our love as we enter into relationship with them and seek to find Jesus in their hearts, God will woo them back to Himself with His unconditional love.

As we have ministered into addiction in America for more than a decade, we have seen that more than 90% of addicts knew who God was. For many of the drug addicts, their first "drug" was being drug to Sunday School by mom or grand mom. However, their hearts had been darkened. "For since the creation of the world His invisible attributes are clearly seen, being understood by the things that are made, even His eternal power and Godhead, so that they are without excuse, because, although they knew God, they did not glorify Him as God, nor were thankful, but became futile in their thoughts, and their foolish hearts were darkened." (Romans 1:20-21)

 Open your heart. See if you can hear the words of any whose hearts had been darkened by the schemes of the Enemy.

"I do this to lose the weight." The words of an addict, when her daughter found her stash in the car console.

"I thought I had it under control, but it had control of me." Crystal, age 21, who was addicted to methamphetamine, had an abortion at age 14, a daughter at age 18, and whose mom is a cocaine and heroin addict.

"It was the hardest boyfriend I ever had to break up with. It's the drug that's addicting. But it's why you start doing it in the first place that's interesting. A lot of it was being a child actor; I learned to suppress feelings." Stacey "Fergie" Ferguson, the female voice of the Black Eyed Peas.[2]

"I was using Ecstasy, a lot of Ecstasy. I had no control. I just did something totally irrational. Believe me, rational people don't go to do something like that in the middle of the day. It's just insane." Amy Fisher, who served seven years in prison for the shooting attack of Mary Jo Buttafuco.[3]

"Everybody gets overwhelmed at points, but it's when you think you can handle it yourself and you don't reach out for help – that is when the end is near. Recognize that you are about to tire, that drowning is looming. I've definitely been the drowning guy, and in the midst of drowning, thought, 'I wonder if I should put my hand up?'" Keith Urban, the Grammy winning country singer, who publicly acknowledged his cocaine addiction and alcohol abuse, discussing the need to speak up to get help.[4]

"The fact is I am guilty of sexual immorality. And I take responsibility for the entire problem. I am a deceiver and a liar. There's a part of my life that is so repulsive and dark that I have been warring against it for all of

my adult life." Ted Haggard, former pastor of New Life Church and president of the National Association of Evangelicals, discussing accusations of his involvement with a male prostitute and methamphetamine.[5]

"Ninety-eight percent of what you knew of me was the real me. Two percent of me would rise up, and I couldn't overcome it." Ted Haggard's words, as stated by Rev. Michael Ware, one of the overseers.[6]

Paul instructs each of us to "Put on the whole armor of God, that you may be able to stand against the wiles of the devil." (Ephesians 6:11) Jesus warns us about the schemes of the devil and states, "The thief does not come except to steal, to kill and to destroy. I have come that they may have life, and that they may have it more abundantly." (John 10:10) God is calling His Church to disciple those whose hearts have been darkened by addiction. God is calling His Church to teach addicts how to stand firm against the devil and his schemes. God is calling His Church to lead addicts into an understanding of the life offered by Jesus Christ so they can be set free from slavery to sin and begin living the abundant life in Christ.

3

The Heart that Yearns for Peace

 In the Kensington section of Philadelphia, the following words are written on the wall of an abandoned home on Sterner Street.

Diary of an Addict
Salvation?
Oct. 6, 2004
3:29 PM
Last high, going to detox, fixing my life and my health... I leave my addiction and old self here. It does feel good to be clean, you just have to get used to it. Whoever reads this, be safe, think about it... remember when we were young, innocent and happy? What happened?   GOO Age 22

March 17, 2005 4:35
If only we chased recovery like we chased that high. Still struggling to stay clean and I'm still —ing up! I need help before it's too late! Heroin already got me Hep C so basically I'm going to have a slow and painful death. Heroin also killed my friend & ruined many things for me! But I still do it. Why? —!   GOO Age 22

Some of us will make it. Will I be one of the few? I have tasted sobriety, and it does taste great. If you pray, please pray for me. I'll be praying for those of you who enter this abandon.   PEACE   GOO

Hopefully I won't be here for another entry...

Can you hear Goo's heart? If you met him on the streets of Philadelphia could you find Jesus is his heart? Goo, like millions of addicts around the world, yearns for a return to innocence and happiness. Questions and uncertainty echo in his mind as he wonders if he will ever make it to the place he prays that all will find, the place of peace.

God is calling His Church to carry His peace into the streets and abandoned homes because "the peace of God, which surpasses all understanding, will guard your hearts and minds through Christ Jesus." (Philippians 4:7) Why is peace so elusive in the midst of addiction? Because the high is counterfeit! It doesn't bring long-lasting peace. It brings instant gratification, which pushes away pain for an instant—only to bring deeper pain and unrest when the high wears off.

Addicts understand their sin as a burden that festers into emotional turmoil. Constantly sick and tired, they live with the pain of rejection by loved ones. The new friends they have in their addiction plan their destruction. But in the wee hours of the morning, when all is quiet, you can hear the soft, sobbing prayers of addicts. With a heart that feels nearly dead, speaking words which feel unworthy of God's ear, the sorrow of the addict is spoken in the darkness.

God hears their cries and understands their pain. When addicts read Psalm 38 they know God understands.

There is no soundness in my flesh because of Your anger, not any health in my bones because of my sin. For my iniquities

*have gone over my head; like a heavy burden they are too heavy for
me. My wounds are foul and festering because of my foolishness.
I am troubled, I am bowed down greatly; I go mourning all the
day long. For my loins are full of inflammation, and there is no
soundness in my flesh. A am feeble and severely broken; I groan
because of the turmoil of my heart. Lord, all my desire is before
You; and my sighing is not hidden from You. My heart pants, my
strength fails me; as for the light of my eyes, it also has gone from
me. My loved ones and my friends stand aloof from my plague,
and my relatives stand afar off. Those also who seek my life lay
snares for me; those who seek my hurt speak of my destruction,
and plan deception all the day long. But I, like a deaf man do not
hear; and I am like a mute who does not open his mouth. Thus I
am like a man who does not hear, and in whose mouth is no
response. For in You, O Lord, I hope; You will hear, O Lord my
God. For I said, "Hear me, lest they rejoice over me, lest, when
my foot slips, they exalt themselves against me." For I am ready
to fall, and my sorrow is continually before me.* (Psalm 38:3-17)

Can you hear the heart of the addict? If you met him in your
neighborhood could you find Jesus in his heart? Can you sense
the burning need for peace in the words of the psalmist?

God is calling His Church to carry His peace to people like
this in our towns, in prisons, and all around the world. Jesus
said, "Peace I leave with you, My peace I give to you; not as the
world gives do I give to you. Let not your heart be troubled,
neither let it be afraid." (John14:27) As we begin relationships
with people entrapped in the tangled turmoil of addiction, they
will see the peace inside of us. As we seek to find Jesus inside
of them, they will feel His peace begin to spring forth from
within, because Jesus is the Prince of Peace.

Countless times as my relationships with addicts grew, they
asked me to talk about my faith, my joy, and my peace. Key in
this development was that I never imposed my beliefs on addicts.
As they saw my heart for them, I earned the right to share my
beliefs with them. My ministry of reconciliation became speaking
the Truth of God's Word in the midst of the lies of addiction.

The prophet Zechariah, in introducing Jesus, says He "shall sit and rule on His throne" and "He shall be a priest on His throne, and the counsel of peace shall be between them both." (Zechariah 6:13) God is calling His Church to speak this Truth to those caught in addiction. All of us, including addicts, need to live a life where Jesus Christ is on the throne of our life.

We must see Him as our King, we must see Him as our Lord, and we must be willing to submit to Him and obey His Word. If I think back to any kingdoms I studied in history classes in school, I recall that anyone disobeying the king ended up in a dungeon or losing his head! Why is it that we find it so easy to rationalize or minimize our actions when we disobey THE King?

We must see Him as our High Priest. As our High Priest, He brings us wisdom and discernment and is our representative to Father God. Why is it that we so easily trust in the wisdom of man, the wisdom of scientists, or scholars? Why is it that we turn to psychics, astrology charts, and fortune cookies for discernment when we are not sure what to do? Addicts deny the Priesthood of Jesus Christ when they self-medicate, by acting out and finding the counterfeit high which allows them to escape their thoughts or pain.

When we do our part in placing Jesus Christ on His rightful throne, His counsel of peace springs forth. This is the same peace that is waiting to spring forth inside the heart of addicts. Are you willing to carry this understanding of Jesus' rightful place to addicts? This truth spoken in love will drive out confusion and deception that has kept many addicts in bondage.

4

The Heart in Need of Forgiveness

 An email excerpt from someone I'll call Debbie:

As you know addicts come in all shapes and sizes, and from all walks of life. Perplexing to everyone that knew of my ad- diction was that I had never done a drug until I was 35. *Stunned me even.*

See Pastor Dave, I was the cheerleader, and homecoming queen. President of my class. Supposedly people wanted to be me. I actually had the nerve to get a divorce because my husband smoked pot. ME!!!!!!

Then it all went bad when I met a guy who was a recovering addict. Seven years of prison. So he was clean. In no way am I blaming that guy for my addiction, but he'd been there. So I became a heroin addict at 35. Plain insanity. I had migraines and this guy kept telling me dope would help. Now I am no dummy. I knew it was dangerous stuff, but I had no idea what it even looked like. Guess what? Men will give or buy you anything to ease your pain. I know that now. He used to just buy it, and give it to me. I didn't have to go with him or have money. It just always was there.

Meanwhile after about six months this guy tried dope. Looking back I think he was doing it all along. One day he was sick, and I just asked him where I go? I was scared senseless getting off at K&A. (An elevated train stop in the Kensington section of Philadelphia.) *You know the rest. It became second nature. I was traipsing around Kensington at all hours.*

So it ended up I hurt everyone I love. My dad never looked at me the same way again. He called me a rotten junkie, and I was a mother, how dare I? I caused the man so much stress. At one point I was trying to get into detox and I had to wait until the next morning. I called my brother who lives close by the detox hospital and asked if I could stay the night. He told me I could sleep in the park. Man that hit me then. I was a cheap, creepy, ugly, skinnie junkie.

A friend of mine who let me kick at his apartment—I robbed him. The day I walked out of detox there were nine of us released all at once. One guy had a car. It was clear they were going to cop. I walked away. One guy yelled to me he had the money for me. I came home and just kept going. So here I am.

Somewhere in me I knew I was still alive when I would be copping in the alley. Children would be in their little swimming pools down in the badlands, and I would just look, and think what a piece of crap I was. I mean nobody should live in that mess, and chaos. Nobody. Walking back to the El I would feel awful because I invaded a neighborhood where people were just like me only raised different. Raised in poverty. God was with me in those times because thank the Lord I was not harmed. That right there is a miracle.

Can you hear Debbie's heart? If you met her on the streets, in an alley, or on a train or bus could you find Jesus in her heart? Would you be willing to walk in the ministry of reconciliation with Debbie and her father? God is calling His Church to lead addicts into an understanding of His forgiveness. God is calling His Church to love addicts so they can forgive themselves. God is calling His Church to lead the families of addicts to be ready to forgive the addicts who hurt them so deeply.

Why is forgiveness such a difficult topic or emotion for Christians to implement in their own life? When we hold onto the hurts and offenses we have felt, they become planted in us growing into roots of rejection, fear of man, and shame. If we allow these roots to take hold, they bear the fruit of anger, blame shifting and defensiveness, escape/isolation and self-medication, fears and phobias, guilt, hard-heartedness, lack of respect and rebellion, low self-esteem/self-image, perfection-ism, the need to succeed and to please people. There are many emotions that fuel an addiction!

What are the words we often say when we are unwilling to forgive? "I can forgive but I can't forget!" "If I forgive that means I am approving of their behavior!" "I do forgive but I don't ever want to associate with them again!" "How can I forgive when they don't ever apologize?"

What does God's Word and His love for us teach us about forgiveness? In the Old Testament Hebrew language, the word for forgive is *salach* which emphasizes God's desire to relieve us of the burden of our offense against Him. The Psalmist wrote, "For You, O Lord, are good, and ready to forgive, and abun-dant in mercy to all who call upon You." (Psalm 86:5)

God is calling His Church to be ready to forgive. Too often when addicts begin their journey back to their earthly family, they find people unready to forgive. This rekindles the guilt and shame which triggers the coping-and-escape mechanism of getting high. Addicts know all too well how their high can numb emotions and pain.

Our Lord Jesus Christ died nearly 2000 years ago to pre-forgive our sins. I can almost hear some of your thoughts now. "But you don't understand how many times I've been hurt by his addiction." "I gave her so many chances in the past, for my own emotional health I can't hope anymore!" Our challenge as Chris-tians is to walk as Jesus did—in an attitude of pre-forgiveness and unable to be offended.

Our hurts and pain, as family and friends of addicts, have often started with us being offended. We've been offended by our hopes and dreams being shattered through their addictive choices and behaviors. Their inability to show love that meets our needs and expectations also offended us.

So how do we begin to not be offended or be less offended? God is calling His Church to follow His example. God doesn't keep track of our wrongs. The Psalmist wrote, "If You should mark iniquities, O Lord, who could stand? But there is forgiveness with You, that You may be feared." (Psalm 130:3-4)

The first step is to not keep track of the wrongs of an addict. We each have a choice. Do you choose to hold on to the offense that hurt you? Can you willingly choose to loose the offense from you before it becomes a deep-seated bitterness?

The second step in following God's example of not being offended is to choose to forget the wrongs of the addict. God chooses to forget our sins. God spoke to the Prophet Isaiah: "I, even I, am He who blots out your transgressions for My own sake, and I will not remember your sins." (Isaiah 43:25) God is calling His Church to grow in His character by choosing to not remember the wrongs that addicts have done.

The third step in forgiveness is to not put reminders of past wrongs in front of addicts when we meet with them. God removes our sin from our His sight. "Indeed it was for my own peace that I had great bitterness; but You have lovingly delivered my soul from the pit of corruption, for You have cast all my sins behind Your back." (Isaiah 38:17) God is calling His Church to follow His example of forgiveness. He is the one who delivers addicts from the pit of corruption. We are called to not rub the past in the face of those who He has delivered.

Throughout the Bible we find many examples of forgiveness: Joseph forgave his brothers who sold him into slavery, Jesus and Stephen forgave those who killed them, and the father's forgiveness of the prodigal son. Spend some time thinking now of those people that you find hard to forgive. Why are you afraid to forgive them? Are you trying to control them through your unforgiveness? Do you honestly believe you need to continue to punish them by withholding forgiveness? Do you realize that unforgiveness is like a cancer inside of you?

Many emotional problems Christians experience are rooted in the realm of forgiveness. When we fail to fully understand and receive God's unconditional love and forgiveness in our own hearts, the enemy is free to torment us in our minds. When we fail to accept God's forgiveness, we become people who are unforgiving of others who have offended us. Again the enemy steps into our minds and we become people who are easily offended, often taking offense when none was meant.

How can you begin the road to wholeness if your life is wrought with anger, bitterness, rejection, shame, fear of man, and unforgiveness? These steps hold true for the addict as well as those hurt by the behavior of addicts.

· First, admit to yourself and confess to God each of the feelings and behaviors which describe you above, then receive His forgiveness and love and forgive yourself.
· Second, admit your faults to someone else and take responsibility for your actions.
· Third, decide if you want to be healed or if you want to remain in your present condition. If you want to be healed, forgive everyone who hurt you and let the love of Christ be evident in your relationships from this point forward. This step involves releasing the other person from their offense and refusing to allow the offense to affect your future relationship.
· Fourth, remove any foothold the enemy may have on you which started when someone hurt or offended you.

Forgiveness is a choice we make. It's your decision. Do you choose to no longer hold an offense against the person who hurt or offended you? Remember, forgiveness does not condone their sin, nor does it give the offender your permission to continue offending.

Forgiveness does free you from the burdens you have been carrying and sets the stage for healing, wholeness, reconciliation, and restoration. If the choice to forgive seems too hard to do on your own strength, tell God that you understand your need to forgive. He is able to touch your heart, transform your heart, and be your strength in the steps of forgiveness.

5

The Heart of Addicts Worldwide

Addiction is a worldwide epidemic. As we traveled to different countries, we found people, churches, societies, and governments trying to deal with the problems of addiction. The common theme was one of hopelessness and helplessness, as no one seemed to have any idea of what would work. Isn't it interesting that hopelessness and helplessness are global themes of those caught in the snare of addiction?

 *"I guess you know I'm a heroin addict?" asked Francois, when I arrived in Johannesburg for a mission trip to South Africa, Swaziland, and Botswana. He had waited for just the right moment, mustering up the courage to broach the subject of his addiction without anyone overhearing.*

You see, Francois was a South African national enrolled in a two-year missionary program. He also happened to be the driver for me and three other people for our five hour trip to Mbabane, Swaziland, after our airplane landed in Johannesburg, South Africa. Making conversation from the front seat of the rental car Francois was driving, I had mentioned, "I work on the streets of Philadelphia with heroin and crack addicts."

Instantly, Francois' demeanor changed, but then he caught himself, changed the subject to South Africa's cricket team and

29

the scenery around us. "Is this your first trip to Africa?" he asked. "Yes, but I hope it's not my last. I'd love to bring my family here to minister. It's awesome to find Jesus inside the hearts of addicts!"

I could tell that I had gone too far with Francois and his driving reflected his emotional turmoil. "Have you lived in South Africa your whole life?" I quickly asked to change the subject. Francois eased back on the gas pedal and let out an audible sigh. "Yeah, I can't wait to share Africa with you guys from the U.S.!"

Three days passed until Francois felt safe enough to share about his addiction with me. "I can tell, the way you look at me, that you know," he said. "How many bags do you do a day?" I asked. "How did you know it was heroin?" Francois asked sheepishly. "Heroin and addiction look the same all around the world," I replied.

"I've been praying, and I believe God sent you here to help me get free from this addiction," Francois continued. "I've tried to stop so many times. I'm down to one or two bags a day but I just can't stop."

As we discussed his history of usage, Francois begged, "Please don't tell the head of my mission group. I know I'd be back using ten or more bags a day if they kicked me out. I can't handle one more rejection."

Looking into Francois' heart, I could see the struggle of an addict who had knowledge of the Truth, but remained in deception. God is calling His Church to lead addicts from the place of knowledge of the Truth to understanding of the Truth which set us free. The difference between knowledge and understanding is the same as the difference Jesus points out after His parable of the seeds, when He says, "He who has ears, let him hear!" (Matthew 13:3-9)

A teachable, hearing heart is essential for the Truth of Jesus Christ to bring freedom. That's why the enemy specializes in confusion and deception! When the Book of Revelation presents the fall of Babylon (the worldly kingdoms), it says "for by your sorcery all the nations were deceived." (Revelation 18:23) The Greek word for sorcery in this passage is *pharmakeia*. This is the same root word for pharmaceuticals. The devil is at his work trying to deceive all nations through pharmaceuticals, drugs, and addictions.

How can we be deceived and teachable at the same time? How can we be deceived and hearing at the same time? The devil knows that we can't! God is calling His Church to step into the gap for those caught in the trap of addiction and deception so they can be lifted to a place in order to hear the Truth.

 The deception of the devil is worldwide! The Lancaster, PA, *Sunday News* reported the following in late 2006:[1]

Russia leads the world, in fact, in a staggering range of scourges and vices.... Russians' propensity to die violently is probably unprecedented in industrialized societies at peace.

What's the reason for such claims as this? Russia's suicide rate at the time of that article was five times that of Britain. Russia's murder rate was 20 times higher than the countries of Western Europe.

There is an obvious culprit: booze, especially the Russian taste for strong spirits, sometimes not fit for human consumption and often moonshine. Heart disease and violence, the two biggest factors in the mortality surge, are strongly alcohol related.

How does this Russian moonshine affect the population? Russia's death rate as a result of alcohol poisoning was about 600 times greater than the United States. One might expect a growing public awareness and an outcry for change with such alarming statistics—instead the population responds with a "grin and bear it" or "I could care less" attitude. This attitude does not change even with the recent growth of HIV infection as a result of, among other factors, alcohol-related reduced inhibitions.

In Irkutsh, which has Russia's highest HIV-infection rate, it shows. Yulia Rakhina, its boss, maintains that attitudes, not cash, are the main obstacle. Young people do not use condoms, she says; even HIV-positive people are blasé. "It's hard to explain to someone who feels well that they're going to die."

Can you hear the heart of addiction in Russia? Can you hear the deception that has Russia in a stranglehold? Whether it is middle-aged men getting drunk on alcohol unfit for human consumption or HIV-infected young people who feel well, the deception is the same. The enemy has blocked their ears to the Truth. God is calling His Church to bring the Truth to Russia and all nations.

 The snare of addiction is expanding in Afghanistan. On January 9, 2006, *Newsweek* magazine reported[2] that Afghanistan's drug trade was threatening the stability of the nation.

A veteran Afghan Interior Ministry official said, "We are losing the fight against drug traffickers. If we don't crack down on these guys soon, it won't be long until they're in control of everything."

The enemy, Satan, comes to rob, kill and destroy. These tactics can readily be seen in the battle of addiction. Hopes and dreams are being stolen, people are dying, and relationships with loved ones are being destroyed all around the world.

Why is it so difficult for governments to win this war on drugs? Money! In Afghanistan the narcotics trafficking industry is $2.7 billion a year. This is more than half of the total economy of Afghanistan. With such staggering amounts of money the lure of corruption runs deep.

If Satan can lure government officials in any country to accept drug money from traffickers, then he robs the people of their trust in leaders, he stirs up violence which leads to more bloodshed, and he destroys the fabric of society. In Afghanistan, according to the United Nations Office on Drugs and Crime (UNODC) and the Ministry of Counter Narcotics, approximately 170,000 people use opium or heroin. Of this number, an estimated 30,000 of the users are female. Both of these statistics are alarmingly high for a Muslim nation.

A Western diplomat in Kabul concluded "Afghanistan's main problems are all linked to drug trafficking: rampant corruption, repressive militia groups, human-rights abuses and bad governance."

Can you hear the heart of addiction in Afghanistan? Can you hear the deception that has Afghanistan, its government, and its future in bondage to drugs and addiction? On August 23, 2006, President Hamid Karzai of Afghanistan was quoted,[3] "If we do not kill opium, opium will kill us." Just as the enemy can end the life of one addict through an overdose, he is seeking to end the existence of entire countries like Afghanistan through dependence on *pharmakeia* for its economy. God is calling His Church to bring the Truth to the addicts, the people, and the government of Afghanistan.

 When my wife and I were on our tenth anniversary vacation in Barbados, we met a man who called himself Doctor on Rockley Beach. As we parked our car in the public beachside lot, Doctor approached us and said, "Smoke... white? I see you're hesitant. It's good, Jamaican buds and powder."
"We're just here to relax on the beach," I said, as I approached Doctor to shake his hand. He shook my hand; then bumped my wife's hand as a sign of respect. After he introduced himself, I leaned closer and in a hushed voice, to show him respect, I told

him about the first "doctor" I met in Philadelphia. "In Philly he was known as the doctor because he would inject heroin into the veins of addicts afraid to do it themselves and those who couldn't find any more good veins on their own," I said.

I shared about our ministry working with people caught in the snare of addiction. Doctor responded, "I used to be addicted, but I don't use any chemicals anymore. Well, a little weed now and then."

I encouraged him to seek the Lord for peace and joy when he felt the need to smoke weed. "Thanks for the encouragement," he said. "I do pray..." You could see his mind drifting off reflectively as he began to walk away. Then he turned back and said, "I have to make a living." We hugged and I prayed as Doctor walked toward the beach to make his living by selling smoke and white to some other tourists.

God is calling us to be His ambassadors whether we're at home or abroad. Are you willing to speak His words of encouragement to someone who could be arrested while you're talking to them?

God is calling His Church to welcome addicts with open arms of love. Too often, when addicts are released from prison or complete a rehabilitation program and show up in church, they are met with raised eyebrows and crossed arms. The welcome that addicts receive is often similar to what Africans with AIDS face when they disclose their condition.

The Lancaster, PA, *Sunday News,* reported[4] the facts regarding social stigmas which people with AIDS must endure in Africa. It's as if we're reliving the era of the scarlet letter, as people are viewed as adulterers, homosexuals, or sexual offenders. As a result of the these judgmental eyes, AIDS patients lose their jobs, friends, and families, and are often driven out of town or sometimes killed.

In 2006, a 15 year old Kenyan boy, whose parents and grandparents died of AIDS, was hacked to death by his only surviving relative, who had forced the boy to live in a chicken coop. In 1998, South African AIDS activist Gugu Dlamini was stoned to death by his neighbors. Tanzanian pastor Amin Sandewa revealed his illness and in 2001 his second daughter died of AIDS. He lost his job as a university chaplain and was sent to Dar es Salaam, where he was promised a new position. As of 2006 he was still waiting, without pay.

"But we don't treat addicts as bad as that!" you're thinking. Are you aware that as many states expand their penalties for sex offenders, some are considering measures like a separate colored license plate so everyone would know if a convicted sexual offender is in the area? In many areas of the country, sexual addicts may have no place to go when they are released from prison. Some are prohibited from going to church by their probation officers because they are not allowed to be anywhere that children congregate.

God is calling His Church to welcome addicts with open arms of love. God is calling His Church to stand up and become advocates for those branded by the legal or medical community as unable to change. God is calling on His Church to trust Him as He changes the hearts and renews the minds of those who were previously caught in the snare of the enemy.

 One of God' new creations, who was rescued from decades of addiction, said in a group session one night:

When you hit bottom, you can stay there and try to die hopeless or you can find hope that there is something better than this addiction which cost you everything.

Can you hear the heart of an addict crying out for hope? If you met him in your neighborhood in church one Sunday morning, could you see Jesus in him? God is calling His Church to be people who carry the love of the Father and the hope of the Son with them everywhere we go. Are you willing to share this love and hope with an addict?

6

The Heart of
Broken Dreams

 Addiction doesn't care who gets caught in its snare. It attacks the young and the old, the rich and the poor, male or female. Jesus said, "The thief does not come except to steal, and to kill, and to destroy. I have come that they may have life, and that they may have it more abundantly." (John 10:10)

The Lancaster, PA , *Sunday News* reported:[1]

Spazz, who said she is 23 (but looks twice as old) said she has been turning tricks on the streets of Atlantic City for five years since arriving from New York. "I really don't want to be doing this," she said. "I want to get my GED and become a child's counselor. But I get sick and I gotta get well."

Bunny, who also works the streets of Atlantic City said "This is no kind of life. None of us graduates from high school thinking we're going to end up doing this."

Can you hear the heart of addicts whose dreams have been stolen by the enemy? Can you hear their battle to break free from the physical and spiritual bondage of heroin? If you met them on the streets could you share the love of the Father and the hope of the Son in the midst of their hopelessness and helplessness?

The Lancaster, PA, *New Era* reported[2] the sentencing of a man who burglarized homes to support his heroin addiction.

The judge who sentenced him to 12 to 24 years in prison stated "I recognize that you had a difficult childhood. However, ultimately, you have to take responsibility for yourself. I think it's somewhat ironic the times you chose to commit these burglaries. While (your victims) were making an honest living, you felt it was appropriate to break in and steal from them."

The defense attorney said his client was remorseful and his actions were motivated by his heroin addiction.

Can you feel the pain of the addict when he listens to the words of the sentencing judge?

Can you feel the pain of the addict as he lives with the reality of 12 to 24 years of his life stolen by the enemy? Could you visit him in prison and share the love of the Father and the hope of the Son?

The newspapers were full of stories of celebrities' battles with substance abuse, addiction and the legal system during 2006. Included in the list were television actors and actresses, radio commentators, professional athletes, movie stars and recording artists. There were stories of DUI's, possession of prescription and illegal drugs, alcohol, bulimia, car accidents, rehabs, court appearances, and time in jail.

Can you hear the heart of people turning to self-medication to handle the stresses of life and celebrity status? If you met them on the street could you speak the Truth to them in love?

Newsweek magazine reported on methamphetamine as "America's Most Dangerous Drug."[3]

 *Terry Silvers is one of the victims of this war. Silvers, 34, worked for 19 years at Shaw carpet mill in Dalton, Ga., dreaming of the day he could open his own body shop. He had a wife, three kids and a 401(k), and he'd never missed more than a few days of work his entire life. A friend talked him into snorting a line of meth to be able to drive home after a few to many drinks. In rapid succession, Terry lost 40 pounds, began having seizures and hallucinations, and quit his job rather than enter a drug treatment program. Ultimately he ended up in jail. "I think meth is one of the plagues the Bible talks about," his wife said.*

Can you see the marriage, the family, the career, the hopes, the plans, and the dreams that the enemy stole from this addict? Can you see the path of destruction that the enemy has planned through enticing people to try meth or other drugs? If you met Terry or someone like him at work or on the street could you hear his heart?

 The Lancaster, PA, *Sunday News* reported[4] that treatment admissions for older adults who became addicted to painkillers and other medications or alcohol rose by 32 percent from 1995 to 2002. These statistics were provided by the Substance Abuse and Mental Health Services Administration (SAMHSA) of the U.S. Department of Health and Human Services. The Pennsylvania Liquor Control Board reported that up to 15 percent of adults over age 65 will develop an alcohol problem after retirement or the death of a spouse.

The use of alcohol or other forms of self-medication can easily become a pattern which stays embedded in us even if we have years of recovery clean and sober. This same article from the Lancaster newspaper described a woman who found herself retired, in her 60's, and an alcoholic. If we look at the pattern in her life, she began drinking in her 40's after she got divorced.

"Depression sets in and you think, to make yourself feel better, you drink. And that got to be a constant crutch for me. I started with wine and my last drinks were vodka."

This habit of drinking away her pain and other emotions continued for years. She would come home from work and use both television and a few drinks as her way to unwind. Just like many others who have experienced the pain of divorce, shattered dreams, and the uncertainty of the future, this type of drinking is an escape from reality which can numb both physical and emotional pain. The next morning however, reality is waiting and added to it are the feelings of guilt, shame, and paranoia.

For this woman the pattern reemerged after retirement and development of the same feelings of loss she had felt with divorce. However, this time it was the estrangement of her daughter and grandchild. Her embedded pattern kicked in just like *déjà vu* as she remembered how to numb the pain and emotions. But without work, her drinking could start earlier each day and last longer.

"I didn't feel like a viable person anymore. I used alcohol to escape, to not feel bad. But the pain was almost intolerable. I felt like I had reached the rock bottom, that there was no where else to go."

Can you see how the enemy killed the emotions of a nurturing mother and grandmother? Can you see how the enemy planned the destruction by introducing something to unwind, which became a crutch and led to intolerable pain? If you met this woman at a senior center, assisted living facility, or in the shopping mall, could you see her heart?

Other stories in the newspaper reveal a broad spectrum of addiction across the population. You can read about college students whose addiction started with a prescription to Ritalin for attention deficit disorder, heroin addicts who overdose from heroin laced with fentanyl, a college student who died of a heart attack after partying with vodka and Red Bull, and teens getting hooked on cold medicines and stealing prescription pills from their parents. What do all of these addicts have in common?

7

The Heart that Feels
Alone, Abandoned
or Rejected

 One thing that addicts around the world have in common is the feeling of being alone. At some point in the life of most addicts, a hurt came as someone who loved them spoke words of condemnation, made them feel abandoned or unimportant, or took away a part of their soul through some abusive action. The reaction to that hurt was to withdraw further, feel more alone, and begin steps toward isolation from friends and family in order to avoid future hurt.

God tells us in Genesis 2:18, "It is not good that man should be alone." God also warns us in 1 Peter 5:8, "Be sober, be vigilant; because your adversary the devil walks about like a roaring lion, seeking whom he may devour." A hungry lion seeks out the wounded, the weak, the young, and the isolated as easy prey to satisfy its hunger.

Can you see how the wounded heart of an addict plays right into the hands of the devil? When the process of withdrawal and isolation begins, the accuser of the saints whispers, "Why tell anyone? No one cares about you." Before long, self-medication becomes the answer to the hurt inside. This self-medication can be drugs, alcohol, sex, lust, pornography, masturbation, anorexia, bulimia, cutting, gambling, or any other impulsive or compulsive behavior which provides an escape from the feelings of pain for the moment.

Soon guilt, shame, deception, and dishonesty make it hard to ask for help. Even when someone sees that something is wrong and offers help, the addict's response is to minimize, rationalize, and shift blame to someone else. Proverbs 18:1 states, "A man who isolates himself seeks his own desire; he rages against all wise judgment."

Larry, writing his life story while incarcerated in Lancaster County (PA) Prison, says:

I grew up with basically my mother raising me alone. There was a couple of step dads along the way, but none of them really had too much of an impact. As I look back on my childhood, it's hard to explain, but I don't remember feeling loved or hated. It seems like I was just there.

Also, when I was real young my mom was having a lot of problems and she had to give me and my next youngest brother up to deal with her problems. Luckily it only lasted two weeks. To this day I battle rejection and abandonment and as I look back I can see the reasons why.

Can you hear Larry's heart and feel his hurt? Would you be surprised if you read the rest of his life story to read about a life of homelessness, addiction to alcohol, cocaine, and heroin, becoming a father before he graduated from high school and the fact that at age 34, Larry is incarcerated in a Pennsylvania State Correctional Facility? Does Larry's life story reinforce the statements that he can never change or that he is a lifelong criminal?

God is the one who speaks love and acceptance to those who feel alone. God is the one who can heal the hurts and change the hearts of men and women that have been labeled as unable to change. This is what

Larry writes from prison in 2007 after that heart changing touch from Jesus Christ.

I'm trying not to wallow in sorrow over my current circumstances. Sometimes I catch myself falling into self-pity and I have to readjust my focus. I know life is not promised to be perfect, but I dislike when I find myself having self-doubt and sometimes remembering past events where drugs and alcohol were involved or past relationships with women. I know all these past events are not pleasing to God.

I know I don't have to dwell on these things. I can do a Bible study, or read the Bible, or pray, or just meditate on the Word and these thoughts will leave me. I see how important fellowship is and to spend time with others praising the Lord and talking and learning, but I also see I need to be solid and know how to be alone and feel the Lord's presence and I do.

The last week or so in my daily devotion the subject has been living above circumstances. Not to be happy about being in jail but to be happy because the Lord is with me through this time. And He is there for me to lean on; He is my strength and my rock, for His mercy and grace, for Him dying on the cross for my sins, for His provisions, food, clothes, shelter. There are just so many things to praise Jesus for and to be thankful for. Most of it has nothing to do with material things so no matter what circumstance I am in I can always find something to thank Jesus for.

Right now as I sit writing this I just want so much to be living out God's plan for my life. I've accepted Jesus in my life and He is who I put my trust and faith in. Even though I don't know exactly what the future holds, I know if I trust in Jesus and make wise, Godly decisions, my life from now on will be fine.

I'm trying to learn how to express my feelings more. I don't want to be a loner any longer. I'll always remember when you told me you loved me. I know that was God's love shining through you. Thank you for your encouragements and teachings. I'm excited to see how the Lord is going to use me.

Can you hear a heart that has been changed by God? What would you do if Larry showed up at your church the first Sunday after he was released from prison? Would you be willing to see Jesus in Larry's heart? Would you offer him housing and a job?

Too often, when inmates are released they are met with caution and fear based on their past and their criminal record. This is especially true if their record includes sexual offenses. I'm not saying, throw all caution to the wind. I am saying God gives us His wisdom, His discernment, and His guidance to be able to welcome anyone into our churches and alleviate the fears of the congregation.

Church leaders are beginning to meet with probation and parole officers to develop guidelines for acceptable supervision of convicted sex offenders in church and at church gatherings. Let's use the name James for the convicted sex offender in this example. These guidelines include such things: as a list of adults in the congregation who are ministering to James in a discipleship role; the agreement that James would arrive at church only with one of these adults, never alone; that James would sit with one of these adults throughout the service as part of their family; that James would never go to the bathroom, water fountain, or anywhere in the church without one of these adults and that James would never enter the Sunday School or youth group areas for any reason, even with one of these adults with him.

We are all God's children. He had plans for each of us as He knit us together in our mother's womb. As God touches the hearts of many men and women in prison, He heals them of the hurt of feeling alone, rejected, or abandoned. These were the hurts that resulted in addiction and imprisonment for many of His children. If He has healed them and they are a new creation in Christ, can you trust Him for their future and open the doors of your heart, your church, and your home to them?

8

The Heart of an Outcast

Feeling like an outcast, a disappointment, the black sheep of the family, or a failure who'll never amount to anything, is a universal feeling of men and women caught in the snare of addiction. In Jeremiah 30:17, God promises, "'For I will restore you and heal you of your wounds,' says the Lord, 'because they called you an outcast.'" These words speak life, healing, and hope into the heart of an addict.

But most addicts struggle with the fear of falling back into their old ways. They have heard from many counselors and psychologists that relapse is one of the symptoms of addiction. God speaks a different message in Jeremiah 3:22, "Return, you backsliding children, and I will heal your backsliding."

Can you hear God's desire to speak truth into the heart of an addict? How could God use you to bring the truth of His love to those who feel worthless, hopeless, and helpless? How could God use you to reverse the impact of hurtful names and labels that were spoken into the heart of His children?

Paul is currently incarcerated in Lancaster County Prison (PA).

I was born in New York City. I had an eye problem at birth and I never felt accepted by anyone. My father died when I was 7 years old. I've been called names my whole life. I always felt stupid because I was always told that I was stupid.

I've only been good at two things in my life, fixing motors and doing drugs. Man, am I good at doing drugs! I am a pro at being a junkie.

My self-esteem has always been low. The more drugs I used, the lower my self-esteem went. I knew everyone saw me as a junkie so I had no remorse in using people to get money to get high.

I would do anything, rob, sell drugs, prostitution, anything to get money for drugs. I loved to get high. When I was high I didn't have to deal with all of my feelings of rejection.

Can you hear Paul's heart and feel the damage done to it by labeling and name-calling? As I got to know Paul in a weekly Bible study inside Lancaster County Prison, my heart would sink every time he started a sentence with, "I'm not as smart as the rest of you," or "I'm not smart enough to understand the Bible as well as everyone else." Forty years after being labeled as stupid, that's how Paul described himself.

Praise God that He sees us as His children fearfully and wonderfully made! Paul has felt the touch of his loving Father and Creator. He now not only reads the Bible out loud in group, but has become an evangelist in his pod in the prison as he invites new inmates to come and check out the Bible study. Paul has been transformed from the label of his youth to an inspiration to me and many other inmates.

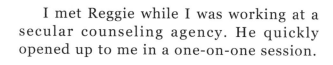 I met Reggie while I was working at a secular counseling agency. He quickly opened up to me in a one-on-one session.

My parents were always fighting when I was growing up. My mom really loves me but I could never do anything to please my dad. He kept telling me I was a no good kid.

But I'm smart and I know how to work. I just have trouble holding a job because of the drugs. I've tried most everything through my teenage years, weed, E, shrooms, angel dust, special K. Right now I'm fighting to stay clean from my latest addiction, heroin.

Reggie stopped coming to counseling and the next time I saw him was in Lancaster County Prison.

I got caught up using crack. Man I never should have tried that stuff. Everything else I seemed to be able to maintain some control, but crack took over in a hurry. I couldn't get enough money to keep up with the addiction.

At age 26, Reggie was sentenced to 25 to 50 years in prison. In less than one month's time, Reggie committed a dozen robberies to support his crack addiction. He pleaded guilty to the knifepoint and gunpoint robberies of a taxi driver; employees at a grocery store, a sub shop, a fast-food restaurant and a video store; three coffee shop clerks and four convenience store clerks.

If you had met Reggie in his teens or early twenties, would you have seen a rebellious youth or a rejected young man? Can you see how the labels and harsh words he endured as a child made him feel like an outcast in his own home? Would you be able to speak words of encouragement, assurance, and hope into this young man's life?

Many of us in church continue the feeling of outcast in men like Reggie with our looks or whispers if they show up for church disheveled or smelling of alcohol. We also separate ourselves from addicts in our prayers as we pray for "them." We pray for God to "wake them up," to "bring them to their senses," to "lock them up to get them to stop."

When Isaiah prayed for his people, he did not pray for "them," he prayed for "us." Isaiah 6:5 says, "Because I am a man of unclean lips, and I dwell in the midst of a people of unclean lips." In Isaiah's Messianic prophecy, he showed us the same attitude would be in Jesus when he says, "And He was numbered with the transgressors." (Isaiah 53:12) Are you willing to be numbered with the addicts? Are you willing to pray as one with unclean lips and unclean hands? Are you ready to stop praying with hands that point fingers at "them?"

God's Word tells us in Psalm 147:2-3, "The Lord builds up Jerusalem. He gathers together the outcasts of Israel. He heals the brokenhearted and binds up their wounds." If you met Reggie or Paul would you be willing to allow the Lord to do His healing and binding through you? God's heart breaks for those who have been labeled, outcast, and rejected. Will you pray for more of God's heart for His precious children? The enemy sits and waits to prey on the outcast in their weakened emotional state!

9

The Heart Holding On to Fear and Pain

 Addicts can identify quickly with the dejection that Jeremiah expressed in Jeremiah 15:18, "Why is my pain perpetual and my wound incurable, which refuses to be healed? Will you surely be to me like an unreliable stream, as waters that fail?" They feel the depth of their own unending pain. After many failed attempts at finding victory over addiction through rehabs, counseling, and other treatment programs, they view God and others who try to help as unreliable streams.

As Paul worked through Step 6 of Alcoholics Anonymous, he expressed sentiments similar to those of Jeremiah.

Do we really want to be rid of our resentments, our anger, our fear? Many of us cling to our fears, doubts, self-loathing, or hatred because there is a certain distorted security in familiar pain. It seems safer to embrace what we know than to let go of it for the unknown.

Can you hear the heart of an addict holding on to pain? Can you see the wicked scheme of the enemy to make pain more comforting than the unknown? Could you speak the Love of the Father and the Hope of the Son into Paul's heart in a way that would bring healing and wholeness. Could you bring the assurance that Paul needs to feel Jesus' healing touch to the depth of his pain?

God's answer to Jeremiah came in Jeremiah 15:20, "They will fight against you but they shall not prevail against you; for I am with you to save you and deliver you." God's heart goes out to those caught in the pain of addiction. His assurance is that He is with us, will save us from the grip of addiction, and deliver us from the hand of the wicked. (Jeremiah 15:21)

 I met Phil at Pike County Correctional Facility. He was serving about a year there before he was returned to the state prison, where he had been incarcerated since 1979. Before he returned to the state prison, Phil shared with me some of his concerns about going back there. Shortly after he arrived at the state prison, he sent me this letter:

Dave, I don't know if you know this or not but I have been with a gang inside for almost 30 years. The brotherhood is not just here but throughout the USA. My rank was a captain.

I really thought I was going to have a lot of trouble my first night in the yard when I went to my crew. They knew I was here before I even got to the yard. A lot of my crew are doing life. I've been with them since 1979. We've been through war together.

But I turned my life over to our Lord Jesus. I told them you are my brothers in the Lord and also my friends, but I can't be in the brotherhood any more. Most of them were okay about it, but there are a few that had smart things to say.

Last night there was trouble in the yard. There are so many people here now and a lot of gang members of all kinds in here. So I will work out in the morning when not as many people are out there, because at night too much trouble happens.

Satan flies around this place let me tell you that! I love the Lord with all my heart and soul. That scumbag Satan! I will be by God's side when He throws him into the pit of fire.

In Phil's words above, can you hear his heart saying, "I joined the gang before I knew the love, comfort, peace, and protection that Jesus could provide. Now that I have Jesus, I don't need the gang." If you met someone like Phil in prison or as a teenager on the streets could you speak God's truth in love in a way that dispels their fear?

I remember seeing the tattoo "NO FEAR" on a young woman nicknamed Shoo in Lancaster County Prison. As she came to know the Lord, I asked her to read 1 John 4:18 which states, "There is no fear in love; but perfect love casts out fear, because fear involves torment. But he who fears has not been made perfect in love." When Shoo came back to group the next week she shared in tears

"My tattoo now has a new meaning to me. I no longer have any fear because of the love I know Jesus has for me. I no longer have anything to prove. For so many years I had to be the tough one to protect myself and my family. Now I know that all that came out of my fear of being taken advantage of. I would hurt others first before they could hurt me or my family."

What an amazing blessing it was for me to watch God transform this tough, young woman into His beautiful daughter! Shoo blossomed over the coming weeks and her tears became a regular event in our Wednesday afternoon groups as Jesus Christ softened her heart. Through a few simple words and the power of the truth of His Word, Shoo was no longer in fear of being taken advantage of if she put her stuff out there in group. Shoo learned that vulnerability with Christ is okay.

Fear can come in a variety of ways. Fear of things, fear of events, fear of man, fear of authority, fear of failure, fear of commitment, fear of responsibility, fear of success, and fear of letting God and others down again. As I've ministered in Lancaster County Prison these past two years, the fear of letting God down again has been voiced repeatedly by men and women getting close to their release date.

Just as the accuser of the brethren, our enemy, Satan distorts our view of our Father God by comparisons to our earthly father, he also distorts the view of God in those who have backslidden before. These inmates who have had their heart touched by Jesus Christ; these inmates who have had their deep inner hurt, which they have previously self-medicated, healed by the touch of Jesus; these inmates who are beginning to feel the freedom, peace and joy that comes as Jesus brings them wholeness and restoration... these are the same inmates whose number one fear is letting God down because they have felt our rejection and seen the hurt on our faces as they have let us down through countless broken promises and relapses.

If these inmates showed up in your church on Sunday morning could you love them? Could you share with them unconditional love which helps them walk in wholeness? Is your walk strong enough to come alongside them and become their friend? These same inmates have heard Jesus call them friend while they prayed on their knees in their 7 foot by 12 foot cell. They have felt Him be the lifter of their heads. Are you willing to allow Jesus to lift their heads through your words of acceptance, encouragement, and love?

Are you ready to change the lofty, judgmental glances, which Casting Crowns sing about in *Does Anybody Hear Her*, into looks of love? Are you ready to risk a broken promise or disappointment from a released inmate to be the hope of Jesus in the flesh for them? They need our trust and vulnerability to see the promise that Christ gave them in a tangible way for their faith to grow into love that has been perfected in a way that casts out all fear. They need the love of the Father and the hope of the Son pouring out through us.

10

The Heart Caught
in Futility

 As you get to know someone caught in the spiritual battle of bondage to addiction, they will be quick to tell you how often they have tried to quit but always failed. Or they'll say, "I've was clean for six months a few years ago, but then I fell back into it." Paul speaks boldly in response to these statements in Ephesians 4:17, "This I say, therefore, and testify in the Lord, that you should no longer walk as the rest of the Gentiles walk, in the futility of their mind."

People caught in futility are caught in a life without purpose. The emptiness that has invaded their mind as a result of repeated failures has stolen their hope of ever getting clean and sober. The words of condemnation as they've been told, "Just stop," "You'll never amount to anything," or "How can you keep hurting your mother and me this way?" have resulted in a ceasing to care about hopes and dreams which seem lost so long ago.

Paul outlines five reasons for this futility of mind in Ephesians 4:18-19:

1) "Having their understanding darkened." By being caught up in the world and conforming to the world's sin, addicts' understanding of God, His love, His power, and their place as His children has been darkened as they abide in darkness.

2) "Being alienated from the life of God." Sin alienates us from God. When we abide in darkness we enter into relationship with the father of lies and even though we may pray, we are separated from the life of God.

3) "Because of the ignorance that is in them." As we spend less and less time in God's word, in fellowship with other believers, and in Bible study or other discipleship, we grow in ignorance of God. Unfortunately, very few churches welcome people caught in the snare of addiction with open arms and even less go out to neighborhoods where addiction is rampant to teach His word.

4) "Because of the blindness of their heart." Hardness of the heart and blindness of the heart is the same thing. Addicts' hearts have been blinded to the love of God by the lifestyle of addiction. It's a lifestyle of deception, broken promises, and taking advantage of everyone for personal gain. If an addict gets totally honest with you, he will admit that his first love is his high. His second love is himself, but at the same time he hates himself more than anything, so the whole concept of love is distorted.

5) "Who, being past feelings have given themselves over to lewdness, to work all uncleanness with greediness." As you talk to drug or alcohol addicts anywhere in the world, you quickly understand how the enemy has gotten them to "give themselves over" to sexual immorality. The link between getting high and needing affection, needing to feel loved, is strong. As men and women caught in the snare of sexual addiction open their hearts to you, they share the battle of shame, guilt, and paranoia as the enemy entangles them in "working all uncleanness."

 In the battle the enemy wages, he robs God's children of their self-worth, he destroys their trust in adults, and thus faithful relationships, and he seeks to kill their hope for the future. Can you hear this battle as Neil shares his heart?

As a young child I was raped by my uncle. I was so young I didn't even know what was really happening. But as this grew into a regular routine of incest I wondered why my parents weren't protecting me! As I reached my years of adolescence, I began to question my role in what had happened. Was I gay? Had that opened the door or invited my uncle into his actions?

I remember feeling so dirty all the time. Slowly, slowly these feelings became something horrible in my mind and I had to escape from them. I turned to alcohol before I turned thirteen. When I drank I had a false courage, a false pride and I felt like I belonged. So I continued to drink more and more as more people accepted me when I was drunk.

But I still had the lingering doubt about my manhood so I turned to sex. If I had sex with lots of girls I could prove my manhood and convince myself that I was not gay. It was easy to have sex with girls if I was drunk and they were drinking too. The escape seemed perfect. I felt like a man, I was accepted and I was loved.

Now here I sit in Lancaster County Prison at age 50 and I realize I don't know what it means to love. I can't relate to a loving father so how do I trust God as my loving Father? I've never had a relationship with someone I could trust. How can I learn to trust God and surrender everything to Him? I've tried so many things that counselors, psychologists and psychiatrists have recommended over the years. I've tried psych meds, behavior modification, cognitive therapy and been treated for dissociative disorder but nothing has worked. Everything ends in futility and frustration. And I still go to sleep every night with worry and fear as I'm riddled with memories that never leave me alone.

Can you hear Neil's heart crying out for love, for self-respect, for meaning in life, for a hope and a future? If you met someone like Neil, could you speak the Truth into his life?

Could you speak the words that bring peace to his mind and soul?

Is Psalm 91 alive in your spirit with words of freedom and assurance for Neil?

Surely He shall deliver you from the snare of the fowler and from the perilous pestilence. He shall cover you with His feathers, and under His wings you shall take refuge; His truth shall be your shield and buckler. You shall not be afraid of the terror by night, nor of the arrow that flies by day, nor of the pestilence that walks in darkness, nor of the destruction that lays waste at noonday. (vs. 3-6)

Could you use the words of Psalm 27 to bring assurance that would birth a declaration of faith in Neil's heart?

The Lord is my light and my salvation; whom shall I fear? The Lord is the strength of my life; of whom shall I be afraid? When the wicked came against me to eat up my flesh, my enemies and foes, they stumbled and fell. Though an army may encamp against me, my heart shall not fear; though war may rise against me, in this I will be confident. (vs. 1-3)
I would have lost heart, unless I had believed that I would see the goodness of the Lord in the land of the living. Wait on the Lord; be of good courage, and He shall strengthen your heart; wait, I say, on the Lord! (vs. 13-14)

Could you lead Neil through John's teachings on the love of God? There are countless Neil's in this world waiting to find the healing, wholeness, and freedom expressed in 1 John 4:18: "There is no fear in love; but perfect love casts out fear, because fear involves torment."

Can you be the arms of Jesus to hug someone like Neil and have him feel the love of God? Can you be the eyes of God and have Neil look at you and see that His Father in heaven loves him?

 Tim is a man I met in prison and later counseled, when he was in a Christian halfway house. He had previously completed more than a year at Teen Challenge, but he was caught in the hopelessness and futility

of never being able to stay clean and sober for more than a few months at a time.

He would be doing well for a few months, but then the thoughts to use would become obsessive and he would find himself compulsively going to a bar for some alcohol, some cocaine, and some sex.

"I guess I'll never be one to make it. I'll always be like this," Tim would say when he shared his remorse after another Friday night relapse. "I prayed and prayed for God to take away my desire to use, but He never does."

Could you minister God's truth if you met someone like Tim on the street, in your neighborhood, or in church? Can God take away Tim's and other addicts' desire to use? Can He take away their cravings and their dreams of using? Of course He can, but often I have found that God chooses to have addicts grow in the knowledge and understanding of Him, so they develop the wisdom and strength needed to resist temptation.

The instruction of Proverbs is sound when ministering to addicts caught in feelings of futility about breaking free from addiction.

My son, if you receive my words, and treasure my commands within you, so that you incline your ear to wisdom, and apply your heart to understanding; yes, if you cry out for discernment, and lift up your voice for understanding, if you seek her as silver, and search for her as for hidden treasures; then you will understand the fear of the Lord, and find the knowledge of God. For the Lord gives wisdom; from His mouth come knowledge and understanding. (Proverbs 2:1-6)

When wisdom enters your heart, and knowledge is pleasant to your soul, discretion will preserve you; understanding will keep you, to deliver you from the way of evil. (Proverbs 2:10-12)

In ministering to addicts, Proverbs 2 continues by promising that when wisdom enters their heart they will be delivered from those:

who speaks perverse things (vs. 12)
who leave the paths of uprightness to walk in the
*   ways of darkness (vs. 13)*
who rejoice in doing evil and delight in the perver-
*   sity of the wicked (vs. 14)*
whose ways are crooked and who are devious in
*   their paths (vs. 15)*
who are immoral woman and seductresses (vs. 16)

 When I met Harry, who was incarcer-
ated in Lancaster County Prison as a con-
victed sex offender, he was eager to get to
know more about God. He came to our
weekly Bible study based on my book,
From Addict to Disciple. In one-on-one
sessions Harry shared that he was a military brat who was never
in one place very long and had lived all over the world.

Before Harry and I had time to identify his feelings which
led to his sexual addiction, he was released from prison. He
had hoped to go to a Christian halfway house, but due to his
conviction as a sex offender and restrictions on closeness to
schools, libraries, etc., he could not go to that program. Out on
his own, within a month he was observed entering a teenage
girl's home several days in a row. He was violated by his probation officer and re-incarcerated. I sat down with Harry the
day after he was re-incarcerated and he expressed his futility
by saying, "I think I'm a Toys R Us kid... I'll never grow up."

Can you hear the hopelessness in the heart of Harry? If you
met him one day could you speak words of truth, assurance,
and encouragement? Could you be his spiritual father and
share Godly wisdom, model Godly decisions, and walk as a man
of God in Harry's life? There are many Harry's around the world
waiting for a Godly man to teach them, lead them, and love
them into manhood. Can you hear God calling you to make disciples?

 I met Bob in Lancaster County Prison. He was caught in the futility of his mind as a result of more than a decade of failures in trying to stop his addiction.

The last time I was released from here I OD'd in less than three hours! I couldn't wait to get high. Now I'm scared to get out. I need a structured environment. I have to move on from my addiction. I have one shot left with Children and Youth to get my son back.

I'm trying to beat the statistics. I'm statistically supposed to fail, but I refuse to let drugs rule my life anymore. I want to feel like a man. I don't want what I had; I want what I hear about.

Can you hear the desperation in Bob's voice? Can you hear the struggle to find the answer to his addiction and to end the futility in his life? Can you hear the heart of a father crying out, to be a father to his son?

11

The Heart in Need
of Fellowship

Isolation is a tool the enemy uses to deepen present addictions and to lead someone back into relapse if they are trying to stay clean and sober. Paul tells us in 1 Corinthians 1:9, "God is faithful, by whom you were called into the fellowship of His Son, Jesus Christ our Lord." The Greek word for this fellowship is *koinonia*. This is a sharing, a close association, a unity brought about by the Holy Spirit. In this fellowship we share a common bond that cements believers to the Lord Jesus Christ and to each other.

Isolation in addiction keeps the addict from relationship with those who truly love him. Isolation in recovery often comes as ex-addicts feel unwelcome at our church; untrusted by their family, friends and employers; or ostracized as probation officers and the court system require that former sex addicts not attend church, for fear of triggering a relapse. The reality is that isolation fuels the enemy to lure people into acting out and relapse.

 I met Ross in Lancaster County Prison. He was incarcerated due to using drugs while on probation for a sex offense. Listen to his heart as he shared his feelings with me.

'I miss my children so much. I can't describe how it feels knowing that I won't be able to see any of my children until

they're over 18 years old. It was my use of drugs that led me into my sexual offense.'

Tears stream down Ross's cheeks as he shares his pain in not being able to be with his family and not being able to have a church family. 'I'm here in this Christian half-way house and I can't go to a lot of activities with the other guys due to my crime. I can't even go out to a baseball game because I'm not supposed to be anywhere that children congregate. I feel like my probation officer is isolating me on purpose to force me into doing something stupid so he can send me back to jail!'

The enemy knows the importance of our fellowship in the gospel and he sows seeds of discord and disunity, as well as court sanctions, to keep God's children in isolation. Paul wrote of the unity God desires through the loving fellowship of believers in Philippians 2:1-4:

Therefore if there is any consolation in Christ, if any comfort in love, if any fellowship of the Spirit, if any affection and mercy, fulfill my joy by being like-minded, having the same love, being of one accord, of one mind. Let nothing be done through selfish ambition or conceit, but in lowliness of mind let each esteem others better than himself. Let each of you look out not only for his own interests, but also for the interests of others.

Can you hear the vital need for fellowship? Can you hear the life-giving strength that comes from the love received in Christian fellowship? Do you remember the cries for love from the voices of addicts in the pages of this book? Do you understand the importance of addicts being in fellowship with believers who can model Christ's character of humility, surrender of self, servanthood, loving our enemies, and building up others?

If you met Ross or someone like him would you be ready to enter into fellowship with him? Would you spend your life on convicted sex offenders hungry for fellowship, hungry for acceptance, hungry for love, and hungry for healing, hungry for wholeness? We are carriers of His truth to help ex-addicts leave behind their walk of darkness and learn to walk in His light.

John outlines the message of speaking the truth in love to show the light to those caught in bondage to sin.

This is the message we have heard from Him and declare to you, that God is light and in Him is no darkness at all. If we say that we have fellowship with Him, and walk in darkness, we lie and do not practice the truth. But if we walk in the light, as He is in the light, we have fellowship with one another, and the blood of Jesus Christ His Son cleanses us from all sin. (1 John 1:5-7)

By first establishing relationship through Christian fellowship, ex-addicts can see that our words come from love, not condemnation. God's heart desires for His children coming out of addiction to be transformed. He wants to give them a new heart and a new spirit. God calls out to them through the words of Ezekiel 18:30-32:

'Therefore I will judge you, O house of Israel, every one according to his ways,' says the Lord God. 'Repent and turn from all your transgressions, so that iniquity will not be your ruin. Cast away from you all the transgressions which you have committed, and get yourselves a new heart and a new spirit. For why should you die, O house of Israel? For I have no pleasure in the death of one who dies,' says the Lord God. 'Therefore turn and live!'

Are you willing to help His children caught in addiction to turn and live? Are you willing to be His ambassador who brings the truth of His promise from Ezekiel 11:19-20?

Then I will give them one heart, and I will put a new spirit within them, and take the stony heart out of their flesh, and give them a heart of flesh, that they may walk in My statutes and keep My judgments and do them; and they shall be My people, and I will be their God.

Are you willing to enter into fellowship and model a lifestyle of Godly decisions? Are you willing to show His love in a way that ex-addicts know that they are His people? Listen to the words of Bob, an ex-addict, who has felt God's healing touch in his heart.

 *Ever since we spoke today, I have been so exhilarated. I knew when I first met you that God put our paths on the same course, but I never could have imagined this to be the outcome. I've always wondered what a man who loves God with everything would be like. Now I know.*

I want so much to learn as much as I can from you. I feel the only way I can ever truly repay you for the freedom you are providing me direction with is to give all the glory to God. For me to be able to talk to you today and reveal the darkest secret that I have carried for 15 years without hesitation blew my mind.

You taught me that God knows all, as I clean up from all the chemicals, God weighed it on my heart heavy that I was doing good, but I still wasn't giving it all up. I knew in my heart I was picking and choosing which parts of God to follow and from your teaching just how ineffective this would be.

This situation is so much more than just me though. My mom and dad, my little sister, my little brother, my sons... I know my parents feel as if they failed in so many ways. I want their exit from this world to be as wonderful as my entrance was for them. I want them to feel like they succeeded in making me the man I am to be. I want to raise my youngest son and get to know my oldest. I don't have a clue how to do this so I am listening to God who is telling me to listen to you.

Can you hear Bob's heart change in his words? Can you hear the cry of a son and a father eager to learn how to be a man of God and make Godly decisions? Can you see the importance of fellowship as God uses us to be His instruments of transformation in the lives of ex-addicts?

Could you teach an addict the truth of 1 Corinthians 10:13? "No temptation has overtaken you except such as is common to man; but God is faithful, who will not allow you to be tempted beyond what you are able, but with the temptation will also make the way of escape, that you may be able to bear it." Could you use this and other Scriptures to encourage an addict to resist the enemy and watch him flee? If you have established fellowship, your enthusiasm for this truth will be contagious!

Listen to the words of another ex-addict who is incarcerated. Listen to hear Landon's new heart and new spirit. Listen to hear the importance of fellowship, feeling loved and accepted, and seeing a model of a Godly lifestyle.

I ask that once this letter is received and opened that, when the time is found, it be read out loud to the whole family. It would be appreciated and bring joy to my heart. Unfortunately, I am currently but temporarily incarcerated on a probation violation.

I stress to the two young men in the family (ages 8 and 10) to never cut themselves short of their future dreams by doing something you will regret and ending up in jail. It is far from a fun place and very painful dealing with being away from your family and friends.

So I encourage you to always do what is right and to keep God in your heart because God is the only one that can keep you away from this place. My prayers are with you...

The reason I am writing this letter is because God put it in my heart to do so. I not only wanted to thank David, but also his family because I know that it is because of the love and support of his family that he is who he is today. David has been a tremendous help to my spiritual growth and has helped me stay on track with God when the devil was trying to push me off.

And from the deepest part of my heart I want to thank him for all of his support. To me he is truly heaven sent. Often times in my Wednesday groups with Dave when he speaks about his family you can feel the love coming off him. Genuinely I feel the love that he has for his family and he created a model for me of what I hope and dream God will bless my family to be.

The other week he showed us the photos of the mission trip to Africa. Those pictures along with the storyline gave me an indescribable hope. One I will carry for the rest of my life.

In conclusion, when I return home one of my main goals is to build real relationships with Christian brothers and sisters. I am a true believer of Christ and strive everyday to become more like Him. A Christian life isn't an easy life, but the reward that awaits us in the end is well worth all that we go through. Let's come together as Christians and praise our creator!

If you met Landon after his release from prison, would you be willing to be one of the real relationships his goal is to build? Would you be willing to be in fellowship with him and help him grow in his Christian walk? Are you ready to come together as Christians with ex-addicts and praise our Creator?

12

The Heart in Need
of Restoration,
Not Rehabilitation

Repeatedly in the Bible, God's love reached out to men and women caught in bondage to sin by restoring them to right relationship with Him. We read throughout the Old Testament of God's people living in captivity, often as a result of their fleshly, self-seeking desires. But God's promise in Jeremiah 24:6-7 for Israel is His promise for His people, His children, His sons and daughters, through the seed of Abraham.

For I will set My eyes on them for good, and I will bring them back to this land; I will build them and not pull them down, and I will plant them and not pluck them up. Then I will give them a heart to know Me, that I am the Lord; and they shall be My people, and I will be their God, for they shall return to Me with their whole heart.

God is waiting to restore His sons and daughters that He knit together in their mothers' wombs. His love is wooing each of them in the midst of their addiction, in the midst of their sin, in the midst of their confusion, in the midst of their despair, in the midst of their hopelessness.

God hears the cries of parents from the deepest depth of heartache as they have watched their children rebel against His ways and get caught in the sinful snare of

65

addiction. He understands their pain. His Words in Jeremiah 31:16-18 and His Spirit reach out to comfort parents and bring hope in the midst of their heartache.

Thus says the Lord: 'Refrain your voice from weeping, and your eyes from tears; for your work shall be rewarded, says the Lord, and they shall come back from the land of the enemy. There is hope in your future, says the Lord, that your children shall come back to their own border.'

In the ensuing verses in Jeremiah 31, Ephraim (Israel) calls out to the Lord in the midst of his chastisement. He likens his time of rebellion as that of an untrained bull. Addicts can identify with this image of themselves as someone puffed up in the deceptive power of their high while truly being out of control the whole time.

God then outlines the steps of repentance, prevention of backsliding, and restoration that we are to follow in order to lead His children in their return to Him. Let's look at the three steps to ministering repentance as outlined in Jeremiah 31:18-20:

I have surely heard Ephraim bemoaning himself: 'You have chastised me, and I was chastised, like an untrained bull; restore me and I will return, for You are the Lord my God. Surely, after my turning, I repented; and after I was instructed, I struck myself on the thigh; I was ashamed, yes, even humiliated, because I bore the reproach of my youth.' Is Ephraim My dear son? Is he a pleasant child? For though I spoke against him, I earnestly remember him still; therefore My heart yearns for him; I will surely have mercy on him, says the Lord.

 The first step of repentance includes a confession of their sin, an assuming of responsibility for their ungodly decisions and actions and a turning to God for forgiveness and to begin to walk in His ways. It is important as we minister to one of God's children

that we don't get caught up in the popular secular approaches or jargon.

Many addicts are hesitant to confess their sins to another person because of some religiosity from their past or from the reality that in the midst of their addiction, they couldn't trust anyone. There is a hesitance based on the fear of betrayal. As Christians we can easily betray the trust of an addict, as we share their situation or circumstances as a prayer request with others in our church or small group.

 The second step is for us to minister His love in the midst of their humiliation and shame as they grasp an understanding of their reproach. It is vital for us at this step to be showing God's love, not tough love. God is beginning to create a new heart in the addict and our heartless actions can wound them. It is typical for addicts to still be dealing with paranoia and our betrayal could restart the feelings of futility or, "What's the use, these Christians are the same as everybody else!"

If you are willing to be open and vulnerable with your past and present struggles, it alleviates the shame the addicts are feeling with their sin. We need to be willing to follow the example of our Father's unconditional forgiveness. Just as God hides our sin behind His back, we need to hide their sinful acts in the midst of their addiction behind ours. If they can look in our eyes and see only acceptance and love, their humiliation will vanish as the dew in the morning sun.

 The third step of ministering into repentance is to help them understand that God's way is love and as we speak correction in love we reassure them of His mercy. We need to remind them that God's heart yearns for them. We need to instruct them on what it means to us to have a Father who loves us unconditionally. We need to

point out that God looks at us and them as His dear son and child who pleases Him.

Jeremiah 3:22 speaks to the depth of God's love and mercy as God says, "Return, you backsliding children, and I will heal your backsliding." This is a mercy that goes way beyond forgiveness! This is God's promise to touch the heart of an addict in a way that heals their heart and makes them whole. As they walk forward in this Truth, they will understand that what was locked inside that they had to keep medicating, has now been healed! Lead them through Jeremiah 3:23 so they can see how they sought in vain to various hills and mountains for something that only God can bring.

Now let's look at the steps to prevent backsliding as outlined in Jeremiah 31:21-22:

Set up signposts, make landmarks, set your heart toward the highway, the way in which you went. Turn back, O virgin of Israel, turn back to these your cities. How long will you gad about, O you backsliding daughter?

 The first step in preventing backsliding is to set up signposts which help us recognize the path that leads to bondage. We need to help people understand as they leave their addiction behind that they need to have glaring reminders, like billboards and neon signs, to bring them to their senses when they are being lured back into their old lifestyle by the wiles of the enemy that look harmless at first.

 The second step is to make landmarks. This speaks to me of the many times the people of Israel built an altar to be a landmark, a remembrance, of what the Lord did for them at that place. We need to help people erect their remembrances of how God saved them, loved them, protected

them, forgave them. An excellent way to do this is to teach them how to journal those times that God has come through for them. Are you willing to share your journal with them as a teaching tool and a faith builder?

 Can you use words of assurance to lead people to the third step of preventing backsliding? This is the step of setting your heart on the highway. We need to help people see the road which leads to salvation and how to set their hearts on walking that path rather than returning to their old ways.

 The fourth step is to help them see that this is a turning back to God's original plan for their life. This is a plan that God has held for them, hidden in Christ since their conception. We need to help them understand that relapse into addiction is a backsliding into bondage to sin and that God is waiting to birth His plan for their life which brings Him glory.

Following the steps repentance and prevention of backsliding, God outlines His heart for restoration in Jeremiah 31:23-34.

 The first step of restoration involves returning to the point of departure from God and His plan for their life. This departure could be either a willful decision or something that was thrust on an individual by someone else. Then addicts need to understand how their thoughts or hurts resulted in sinful actions, decisions to self-medicate, and captivity to sin. But God promised a return of normalcy in the lives of addicts as He said, "I have fully satisfied the weary soul, and I have replenished every sorrowful soul." (vs. 25)

 Our step of ministry is vital as we work with addicts to come to an understanding of the hurt, pain, rejection, betrayal, abandonment, disappointment, fear, or whatever it was that led to their steps of departure from God and the beginning of self-medication to deal with or escape from that pain. Then part of the replenishment they feel from God is a restoration of joy, peace, hope, faith, and trust that He loves them and will never forsake them. God's promises are an effective tool in ministering at this point of restoration.

> *I will watch over them to build and to plant, says the Lord. (vs. 28)*
> *I will make a new covenant. (vs. 31)*
> *I will put My law in their minds, and write it on their hearts; and I will be their God, and they shall be My people. (vs. 33)*
> *For I will forgive their iniquity, and their sin I will remember no more. (vs. 34)*
> *Behold, I am the Lord, the God of all flesh. Is there anything too hard for Me? (Jeremiah 32:27)*
> *Call to Me, and I will answer you, and show you great and mighty things, which you do not know. (Jeremiah 33:3)*
> *Behold, I will bring it health and healing; and I will heal them and reveal to them the abundance of peace and truth. (vs. 6)*
> *I will cleanse them from all their iniquity by which they have sinned against Me, and I will pardon all their iniquities by which they have sinned and by which they have transgressed against Me. (vs. 8)*
> *For I will cause the captives of the land to return as at the first, says the Lord. (vs.11)*

In summary, how do we minister God's gift of restoration in a society focused on rehabilitation, incarceration, behavior modification, and prescription medications to keep people from acting out? Again, the steps are repentance, prevention of backsliding, and restoration. We are called to this ministry in James 5:19-20: "Brethren, if anyone among you wanders from the truth, and someone turns him back, let him know that he who turns a sinner from the error of his way will save a soul from death and cover a multitude of sins." Are you ready to walk in this ministry? Are you ready to see those in prisons, in abandoned homes, in hopelessness, in helplessness, as God's children "among you"?

The following poems were written by inmates who found the gift of God's love and restoration.

He Calls Us By Name
by A. B. Liever

I've heard my name so many times,
In the darkness, oh so blind.
I've seen my face, I know it's mine,
It looks away all the time.

I hear my name, my Father calls me,
He wants me to meet at Calvary.
I'm so unworthy, full of shame,
My Father calls me, all the same.

I walked up that hill and looked up at the cross,
My heart in my throat, words at a loss.
I sank to my knees on that Holy hill,
Repented and prayed and gave up my will.
Lead me, guide me, show me the way,
For narrow it is, and I don't want to stray.
Praise be to God our Father above,
And our Lord Jesus Christ our Savior of Love.

Deep Feelings
by Shawna L. Luzier

I lay here and think to myself
What would make me happy?
Peace, love, self-esteem, freedom
Happiness itself?

But how do I find it?
Where do I look?
People around me already think
I'm cocky, confident, happy, free in my own way
And at peace with what is going on in my life.
I'm not.

My life is like a game of charades,
One day I pretend I can be at peace
But inside I'm crying out for help.
Where to turn? Who to confide in?

The next time I'm this vain, proud woman
But inside I'm ugly, dirty and scorned.
How to change? Am I? Really?
Am I even liked?
I mean the true me?
Whoever that may be.

These voices I hear are they different Shawnas
Wanting a chance to come out?
My different personalities
Is that a different version of me; but me?

A lot of questions, no answers, anywhere!
I'm lost inside myself turning in all and every direction.
Slowly I'm dying and running out of places to go.
No help, no truth behind people's answers

And doors they try to open.
It's just me lost among both worlds
Yours and mine...

A new day has occurred,
For I found my way to the Lord.
He has given me the light,
To finally want to change my life.
I want to try something new,
I'm on my way to Bethesda
To do follow through.

Avoid the liars, false prophets, even the deceitful fights.
God and I are as one!
I feel wonderful to be His new found daughter!
God loves all of us, just give Him a chance.
He'll change you too, with the work of His almighty hands.
Pray, read your Bible, and follow 1 Corinthians 15:33
God was and is the only One to set you free!

The Lord's Love
by Gregory Williams

The Lord's love surpasses
Any love you'll know.
He gently placed you in the womb
And lovingly watched you grow.
Before you knew yourself
He patiently numbered your hair.
And kept His watchful eye on you
To show you He really cares.

He comforted you for days on end
When you felt that no one else would.
He held you tightly in His arms

Like only the true Father could.
He'll never stop encouraging you
To keep you going strong.
Not to mention the peace of mind you'll have
In knowing you belong.

He's looking down from heaven upon you
With a smile as bright as the sun.
Holding a scroll with the inscription that reads:
"I'm pleased my child, well done."

P.S. Inspired by God

Footnotes

Chapter 1
[1] Lancaster (PA) *New Era*, October 26, 2006.

Chapter 2
[1] Excerpt from a tract, Gospel Tract Society, Inc., Independence, MO.
[2] "Singer tells of breaking addiction," Lancaster (PA) *New Era*, September 11, 2006.
[3] "The agony of Ecstasy," Lancaster (PA) *New Era*, April 28, 2006.
[4] "Keith Urban has advice," Lancaster (PA) *New Era*, November 9, 2006.
[5] "'I am a deceiver and a liar,'" Lancaster (PA) *New Era*, November 6, 2006.
[6] "Haggard's own rules sealed his fate," Lancaster (PA) *New Era*, November 19, 2006.

Chapter 5
[1] "A national sickness of the soul?" Lancaster (PA) *Sunday News*, October 1, 2006.
[2] As reported in *Newsweek,* January 9, 2006, in the article "A Harvest of Treachery" by Ron Moreau and Sami Yousafzi.
[3] "New anti-drug policy," Lancaster (PA) *New Era*, August 23, 2006.
[4] "Clergyman with HIV raises some eyebrows," Lancaster (PA) *Sunday News*, May 7, 2006.

Chapter 6
[1] "Hookers easy prey in Atlantic City," Lancaster (PA) *Sunday News*, December 3, 2006.
[2] "Burglar sentenced to 12-24 years in jail," Lancaster (PA) *New Era*, July 19, 2006.
[3] As reported in *Newsweek,* August 8, 2005, in the article "America's Most Dangerous Drug," by David J. Jefferson.
[4] As reported in the Lancaster (PA) *Sunday News*, June 5, 2005.

About the Author

Rev. Dr. David L. Hain and his wife Shawn served through Adventures in Missions (Adventures.org), bringing the love of the Father and the hope of the Son to addicts, the poor, and the homeless. Dave received his Doctorate of Ministry from Faith Covenant Theological Seminary (fccca.org) in Palm Harbor, Florida.

Dave is the founder and executive director of 'Etsah Ministries (EtsahMinistries.org) based in Quarryville, Pennsylvania. 'Etsah Ministries is bringing the Truth to the world that the battle against addiction of any kind is a spiritual battle. The vision of 'Etsah Ministries is to equip the Body of Christ to bring wholeness, healing, reconciliation, and restoration to individuals, families and communities torn apart by substance abuse, other addictions, and dependence on prescription drugs.

Dave has traveled around the United States and to Europe, Asia, Africa, and the Middle East, sharing his vision for God's heart for addicts. If you are interested in hearing Dave speak; assistance in starting addictions ministry in your church, prison, school, workplace, or community; or need advice on a family intervention situation, please contact: david.hain@gmail.com

COACHWHIP PUBLICATIONS

Also Available,

From Addict to Disciple
David L. Hain

ISBN 1-930585-22-5

CPSIA information can be obtained
at www.ICGtesting.com
Printed in the USA
BVHW01s0932010318
509312BV00001B/10/P

9 781930 585430